find
your
calm.

This edition first published in Great Britain in 2024
by SJG Gift Publishing, HP22 6NE.

Author: Sasha Morton
Design: Bag of Badgers Ltd.
ISBN: 978 1 915902 71 9
Printed in China
10 9 8 7 6 5 4 3 2 1

Welcome to **Find Your Calm** – a collection of **advice–led quotes** that will help you deal with **whatever challenges life throws at you**. These wise, and often wryly humorous words, recommendations, and shared experiences prove that we all need to slow down and take a moment to reset from time to time. So, unclench your jaw, drop your shoulders, take a deep breath and let each page help you relax and unwind.

Enjoy!

For fast–acting relief,
try
**slowing
down.**

Lily Tomlin

Rule number one is
   DON'T SWEAT THE
   SMALL STUFF.
Rule number two is that
   IT'S ALL
   SMALL
   STUFF.

Robert Eliot

The less you respond to negative people, the more **peaceful** your life will become.

Unknown

Breathe.
Let go.
And remind yourself
that this very moment
is the only one you
know you have for
sure.

Oprah Winfrey

Your mind
will answer
most
questions if
you learn
to relax and
wait for the
answers.

William S Burroughs

You may not
control all
the events
that happen
to you, but you
can decide not
to be reduced
by them.

Maya Angelou

Life goes by fast.
Enjoy it.
Calm down.
It's all funny.
Next.

Joan Rivers

Sometimes I wish I could go into a time machine right now and just look at myself and say,

'Calm down. Things are gonna be fine. Things are gonna be all great. Just relax.'

Tristan Wilds

If we take care of the moments, the years will take care of themselves.

Maria Edgeworth

Calm mind
brings inner
strength and
confidence.

Dalai Lama

How beautiful it is to do nothing, **and then to rest afterwards.**

Spanish Proverb

There is
peace
even in
the storm.

Vincent van Gogh

I am a
   BLANK SLATE –
therefore
   I can create
   ANYTHING
      I WANT.

Tobey Maguire

I pray to
be like the ocean,
with soft currents,
maybe waves at times.

More and more,
I want the consistency
rather than the
highs and the lows.

Drew Barrymore

It is possible to experience an awakening in this life through realising just

how precious
each moment,
each mental process,
and each breath
truly is.

Christy Turlington

Follow your instincts and do not let other people's opinions of you become your opinion of yourself.

Sarah Jessica Parker

Taking time to sit back and watch and think about what you've seen is important. Travelling did a great deal to me. I found that when I travel and just sit in the corner and watch, a million ideas come to me.

Lionel Richie

Let go of
the thoughts
that **don't**
make you
strong.

Karen Salmansohn

Make peace
with your
mind:
it's
your
best
ally.

Unknown

The
challenge
is not to
be perfect –
it is
to be
whole.

Jane Fonda

Until you value yourself, you won't value your time.

Until you value your time, you will not do anything with it.

M Scott Peck

Mindfulness can help people of any age. That's because we become what we think.

Goldie Hawn

You either listen to the naysayers and fall into the pit of self-loathing,

or

you stay on the path and move forward.

Chris Pine

My philosophy is it's none of my business what people say of me and think of me. I am what I am, and I do what I do. I expect nothing and accept everything. And it makes life so much easier.

Anthony Hopkins

Unknown in Paris, I was lost in the great city, but the feeling of living there alone, taking care of myself without any aid, did not at all depress me.

If sometimes I felt lonesome, my usual state of mind was one of calm and great moral satisfaction.

Marie Curie

I restore myself when I'm alone.

Marilyn Monroe

I love to have a bath with beautiful, relaxing music on and have no rush to do anything.

It's a wonderful indulgence, and it helps me to calm down and stop my mind running overtime.

Kylie Minogue

As important as it
is to have a plan
for doing work,
it is perhaps more
important to have
a plan for rest,
relaxation,
self-care
and sleep.

Akiroq Brost

I think every individual has his or her own power, and it's a matter of working, taking time and defining what that power is.

Jill Scott

Don't let
people pull
you into their
storm.
Pull them
into your
peace.

Kimberly Jones

Peace begins with a smile.

Mother Teresa

Keep Calm and Carry On.

George Orwell

When people ask me what the most important thing is in life, I answer 'JUST BREATHE'.

Yoko Ono

90% of what you're stressing about right now won't even matter a year from now.

TAKE A DEEP BREATH.

Mel Robbins

Self-care is giving the world the best of you, instead of what is left of you.

Katie Reed

The ideal of calm exists in a sitting cat.

Jules Renard

Just when you feel you have **no time to relax,** know that this is the moment you most need to **make time to relax.**

Matt Haig

Look deep into
nature, and
then you will
**understand
everything
better.**

Albert Einstein

I would have thought that
I would have become one
of those parents – **just
because it's my nature to
be such a perfectionist** –
that anything falling short, I
would have seen as a failure.

But something has happened
to me over the past few years
– **it's not Zen, believe me,
I'm not at all Zen** –
but I'm so appreciative of
even the chaos.

Brooke Shields

It is only in
our decisions
that we are
important.

Jean-Paul Sartre

Tension is who
you think you
should be.

**Relaxation is
who you are.**

Chinese Proverb

If I could
give my
teenaged self
any advice,
it would be
'CALM DOWN!'

Zooey Deschanel

The best thing one can do when it's raining is to let it rain.

Henry Wadsworth Longfellow

One of the lessons that I grew up with was **to always stay true to yourself** and never let what somebody else says distract you from your goals. And so, when I hear about negative and false attacks, I really don't invest any energy in them, because **I know who I am.**

Michelle Obama

We make
a living by
   what we get,
but we make
a life by
   what we give.

Winston Churchill

Try
to
be
a
rainbow
in
someone's
cloud.

Maya Angelou

I can have
as many
bad days
as anyone.
But I choose
to say,
'I'M JUST FINE.'

Mary J Blige

You cannot control what happens to you, but you can control your attitude toward what happens to you, and in that, you will be mastering change rather than allowing it to master you.

Brian Tracy

I've realised that
I am who I am
and that is it.
Like it or lump it,
I'm not around
to please anyone
anymore, and it's a
huge relief.

Kristin Scott Thomas

Surfing soothes me.
The ocean is so
magnificent,
peaceful,
and awesome.
The rest of the world
disappears for me when
I'm on a wave.

Paul Walker

The older you get, the more 'mindfulness' becomes about trying to remember why you came upstairs.

Victoria Coren Mitchell

If I want to **calm down**, I'll buy some fabric, get a pattern, shut myself in a room and stay there for days, really happy. And at the end of it, you get a bedspread or some curtains or something to wear – **it's lovely**.

Twiggy

There are
always
flowers for
those that
want to
see them.

Henri Matisse

For my part,
**I know
nothing with
any certainty,**
but the sight
of the stars
makes me
dream.

Vincent Van Gogh

If you cannot
   find peace
      within yourself,
you will
   never find it
      anywhere else.

Marvin Gaye

The thing you fear
most has no power.

Your fear of it
is what has
the power.

Facing the
truth really will
set you free.

Oprah Winfrey

Holding on to anger is like grasping a hot coal with the intent of throwing it at someone else; **you are the one who gets burned.**

Buddha

Yesterday is ashes, tomorrow wood. ONLY TODAY DOES THE FIRE BURN BRIGHTLY.

Eskimo Proverb

The high
road and
positivity is
never the
easy way, but
**always the
best way.**

Nancy Wilson

It's okay to take time for yourself. We give so much of ourselves to others and we need to be fuelled both physically and mentally. If we are in balance, it helps us in all our interactions.

Faith Hill

Yesterday's the past, tomorrow's the future, but today is a gift. That's why it's called the present.

Bill Keane

HORSES CALM ME.

I love being
around them.
They smell great,
they are beautiful
to look at,
they are loving,
demanding,
temperamental,
and they
settle you.

Shania Twain

There is
no such thing as aging,
but maturing
and knowledge.

Celine Dion

If you do what you love, it is the best way to relax.

Christian Louboutin

When you arise
in the morning,
think of what
a precious
privilege it is
to be alive –
    to breathe,
    to think,
    to enjoy,
    to love.

Marcus Aurelius

For me,
training is
my meditation,
my yoga,
hiking,
biking
all rolled into one.

Dwaye 'The Rock' Johnson

Give
your
stress
wings
and let *it fly away.*

Terri Guillemets

When everything seems to be going against you, remember that the airplane takes off <u>against</u> the wind, not with it.

Henry Ford

Peace cannot be kept by force; it can only be achieved by understanding.

Albert Einstein

Never let success get to your head, and never let failure get to your heart.

Drake

It's okay to
be flawed
because that's
what makes
me … me.

Demi Lovato

There are
two ways of
spreading light:
to be the
candle or the
mirror that
reflects it.

Edith Wharton

You are the
one thing
in this world,
above all other things,
that you must
NEVER GIVE UP ON.

Lili Reinhart

One day, **you'll find your tribe**. You just have to trust that people are out there waiting to love you and celebrate you for **who you are**.

Wentworth Miller

People are often afraid to admit difficulties, but I don't believe there should be a struggle with anything that's the truth.

Harry Styles

Taking time to do something slower than you normally would is a privilege that should not be ignored.

Harper Reed

Don't let yesterday take up too much of today.

Will Rogers

The only
way to find
true peace
is to start
by finding
peace within
yourself.

Unknown

Your living is
determined not
so much by what
life brings to you
as by the attitude
you bring to life;

not so much by
what happens to
you as by the way
your mind looks
at what happens.

Khalil Gibran

I feel like if you're a really good human being, you can try to find something beautiful in every single person, no matter what.

Lady Gaga

We all get so caught up in our day-to-day lives and have so many gripes. But when you see the way others live and how they make the best of it, you'll realize how lucky you are.

Kristin Davis

I wouldn't change a thing about what I've done in the past, **because what may have been bad choices have all led me to this moment.**

Minnie Driver

Rivers
know
this:
there
is
no
hurry.
We
shall
get
there
someday.

A A Milne

When you realise how perfect everything is, you will tilt your head back and laugh at the sky.

Buddha

Definitely trust yourself.
Work hard.
Be honest with yourself.
And life can be joyful.
It is joyful.
Just give it your all,
and it's all going to
work out.

Katie Holmes

Reflecting
on where
I came from
helps me to
appreciate
and balance
what I have
now.

Meghan Markle

When a woman becomes her **own best friend,** life is easier.

Diane Von Furstenberg

Meditation
or going for
a walk, being
kind to your
body …

Those little
things make
a difference
ultimately.

Dakota Johnson

In the midst
of movement
and chaos,
keep stillness
inside of you.

Deepak Chopra

My breakthrough came when I stopped feeling sorry for myself and took responsibility for every part of my life. No more pity parties. I've gotta love me more than anybody else loves me.

Mary J Blige

Any time
I am nervous,
I do a couple of
yoga breaths,
and I am fine.

Jaimie Alexander

The more you trust
your intuition, the
more **empowered
you become,**
the **stronger**
you become, and
the **happier** you
become.

Gisele Bundchen

You owe it
to yourself
to live
beautifully.
And I am.

Jill Scott

Keep your face always towards the sunshine – and shadows will fall behind you.

Walt Whitman

Everyone deals
with some kind of
anxiety or pressure.
WE'RE ALL
IN IT TOGETHER.

Shawn Mendes

Maybe they will choose you and maybe they won't.
But _none_ of it matters if you choose yourself.

Karen Salmansohn

Choose
people
who
will
lift you up.

Michelle Obama

I don't belong
to anyone else
but myself.
I have to make my
own decisions.
HAPPINESS IS
DEFINED BY ME.

Keke Palmer

There is only
one happiness
in this life,
to love
and
be loved.

George Sand

There are
two places
where I can
**completely
relax:**
in nature and
by the piano.

Sigrid

If you have
a garden
and a library,
you have
EVERYTHING
you need.

Cicero

Flowers are
restful to
look at.
They have
neither emotions
nor conflicts.

Sigmund Freud

Chaotic people often have chaotic lives, and I think they create that.

But if you try and have an inner peace and a positive attitude, I think you attract that.

Imelda Staunton

Your community
– no matter who it is –
can help you find balance!
Don't expect yourself
to be a superhuman!
It's just not possible.

Kate Hudson

One thing that has become abundantly clear to me … over the years is the innate power we each have within us to establish deep connection with one another and heal ourselves simply by sharing our stories.

Christy Turlington

Always have an attitude of gratitude.

Sterling K Brown

If you want to relax, watch the clouds pass by if you're laying on the grass, or sit in front of the creek; just doing nothing and having those still moments is what really rejuvenates the body.

Miranda Kerr

Start where you are.
Use what you have.
Do what you can.

Arthur Ashe

Stop a minute,
right where you are.
Relax your shoulders,
shake your head
and spine like a dog
shaking off cold water.
Tell that imperious
voice in your head to
BE STILL.

Barbara Kingsolver

To plant a
garden is to
dream
of
tomorrow.

Audrey Hepburn

There is
always a
sunrise
and always
a sunset
and it's
up to you
to choose
to be there
for it.

Cheryl Strayed

You can't connect the dots looking forward; you can only connect them looking backwards. So, you have to trust that the dots will somehow connect in your future. You have to trust in something – **your gut, destiny, life, karma, whatever.**

Steve Jobs

I am happy
because
I'm grateful.

I choose to
be grateful.

That gratitude
allows me
to be **happy**.

Will Arnett

Never continue in a job
you don't enjoy. If you're
happy in what you're
doing, you'll like yourself,
you'll have inner peace.
And if you have that,
along with physical health,
you will have had more
success than you could
possibly have imagined.

Johnny Carson

Life itself
is the most
WONDERFUL
FAIRY TALE.

Hans Christian Andersen

Cleaning is my **favourite way to relax**.

I clear things out and get rid of the stuff I don't need.

When the food pantry and the refrigerator are organized, **I feel less stressed**.

Jennifer Morrison

Truly appreciate those around you, and you'll soon find many others around you.

Truly appreciate life, and you'll find that you have more of it.

Ralph Marston

Your mind knows only some things.

Your inner voice, your instinct, knows everything.

If you listen to what you know instinctively, it will always lead you down the right path.

Henry Winkler

Be thankful for what you have; you'll end up having more.

If you concentrate on what you don't have, you will never, ever have enough.

Oprah Winfrey

I did this scene in *Lars and the Real Girl* where I was in a room full of old ladies who were knitting.

They showed me how. It was one of the most relaxing days of my life.

If I had to design my perfect day, that would be it.

Ryan Gosling

I used to get stressed out all the time when I thought winning was important.

I wanted to try to win and help my kids win.

Once I figured out it wasn't about winning or losing, it was about teaching these kids about being men, that's when I started to relax.

Snoop Dogg

The time
you enjoy
wasting
is not
wasted time.

Bertrand Russell

I think it's
    my adventure,
     my trip,
       my journey,

and I guess
my attitude is,
     let the chips
     fall where
     they may.

Leonard Nimoy

Life flies by, and it's easy to get lost in the blur.
In adolescence, it's
'How do I fit in?'
In your 20s, it's
'What do I want to do?'
In your 30s,
'Is this what I'm meant to do?'
I think the trick is living the questions. Not worrying so much about what's ahead but rather sitting in the grey area –
being OK with where you are.

Chris Pine

I am my
own sanctuary
and I can be **reborn**
as many times as I
choose throughout
my life.

Lady Gaga

Some **old–fashioned** things, like **fresh air** and **sunshine** are hard to beat.

Laura Ingalls Wilder

Musicians want to be **the loud voice** for so many **quiet hearts.**

Billy Joel

Be yourself – it's the
inner beauty that counts.
You are your
own best friend,
the key to your own
happiness,
and as soon as you
understand that
– and it takes
a few heartbreaks –
you can be happy.

Cherie Lunghi

There's nothing like taking Proust to the beach and daydreaming along with it.

Jerry Hall

I get those fleeting, beautiful moments of inner peace and stillness – and then the other 23 hours and 45 minutes of the day, I'm a human trying to make it through in this world.

Ellen DeGeneres

Look at a tree, a flower, a plant. Let your awareness rest upon it. How still they are, how deeply rooted in Being. Allow nature to teach you stillness.

Eckhart Tolle

There's no shame in enjoying a quiet life. And that's been the realization of the past few years for me.

Daniel Radcliffe

My quest these days is to find my long-lost inner child, but I'm afraid if I do, I'll end up with food in my hair and way too in love with the cats.

Kenny Loggins

The best
cure for
the body
is a
QUIET MIND.

Napoleon Bonaparte

I have insecurities of course, but I don't hang out with anyone who points them out to me.

Adele

I've made a lot of money, but I want to enjoy life and not stress myself building my bank account.
I give lots away and live simply, mostly out of a suitcase in hotels.

Keanu Reeves

Old age
is just a
record
of one's
whole life.

Muhammad Ali

I am
very content.
I like the
kind of person
that I am.

Dolly Parton

I've come to a realization
that I need to be able to
forgive myself for
making the wrong choice,
trusting the wrong person,
or figuratively falling
on my face in front of
everyone.
STEP INTO THE
DAYLIGHT AND
LET IT GO.

Taylor Swift

This is a new me,
this is an older me,
this is a thicker me,
this is a wiser me,
this is a thankful me.

Tyra Banks

Inner silence promotes clarity of mind; It makes us value the inner world. It trains us to go inside to the source of peace and inspiration when we are faced with problems and challenges.

Deepak Chopra

I firmly
believe that
nature brings
solace in
all troubles.

Anne Frank

You really have
to look inside
yourself and find
your own inner
strength, and say,

'I'm proud of what
I am and who I am,
and I'm just going to
be myself.'

Mariah Carey

No book is just
one chapter.

No chapter tells
the whole story.

Keep turning the
pages that need
to be turned.

Angel Chernoff

Be careful who you follow on social media. Anyone who triggers you or makes you feel bad about yourself, unfollow those people, you don't need those thoughts in your brain.

Jameela Jamil

Challenge yourself to paint or draw a series of five pictures a day — it allows you to be loose and a little sloppy and get you out of a perfectionist mindset.

Lena Dunham

The earlier you learn
that you should focus on
what you have,
and not obsess about
what you don't have,
the happier you will be.

Amy Poehler

One of the reasons I overschedule myself is my lifelong pal, _anxiety_. I know I'm not alone and more importantly, to all those like me who overschedule, overthink, overwork, over–worry and over–everything, please know you're **not alone**.

Ryan Reynolds

Those who
contemplate
the beauty of
the earth find
reserves of
strength that will
endure as long
as life lasts.

Rachel Carson

I feel
<u>very comfortable</u>
in my own skin ...
I'm right where
I should be.

Amy Schumer

If I'm ever feeling
tense or stressed
or like I'm about to
have a meltdown,
I'll put on my iPod
and head to the gym
or out on a bike ride.

Michelle Obama

I find a certain
peace by thinking of
me in public as sort
of an avatar self.
You out there can
have the avatar me.
I can keep me.

Jennifer Lawrence

The power
of finding
beauty in
the humblest
things makes
home happy
and life lovely.

Louisa May Alcott

Your self-worth
is determined
by you.

You don't have
to depend on
someone telling
you who you are.

Beyoncé

Be selective in
your battles.
Sometimes peace
is better than
being right.

Unknown

Music
is
healing.

Prince

I take a bath
every single night.

I got really into taking them
when I was 22 and shooting
Emma in London.

I fell in love with the ritual
of it – lighting a candle
and having a cup of tea or
a whiskey, depending on
the day. It's non–negotiable.

I just need that time,
so I take it.

Gwyneth Paltrow

I never look back, darling. It distracts from the now.

Edna Mode

Sometimes the most important thing in a whole day is the rest we take between two deep breaths.

Etty Hillesum

Don't underestimate the value of doing nothing, of just going along, listening to all the things you can't hear, and not bothering.

A A Milne

I promise you,
the gym has taken
away so much of
my stress.
It has helped
calm me down.
When I'm fidgety
and I just feel
like everything is
closing in,
I go to the gym.

Khloe Kardashian

Whatever happened to you in your past has no power over this present moment, because life is now.

Oprah Winfrey

Let's practice
**MOTIVATION
AND LOVE,**
not

**DISCRIMINATION
AND HATE.**

Zendaya

You can do anything as long as you don't stop believing. When it is meant to be, it will be. You just have to follow your heart.

Keke Palmer

I find **meditation** in sitting on the floor with the **kids colouring for an hour**, or going on the **trampoline**.

Angelina Jolie

Peace is its own reward.

Mahatma Gandhi

On a motorcycle, you can't really think about more than where you are.

There's a freedom that comes from that – from stress, worry, sweating the small stuff.

Laurence Fishburne

I put my headphones in and just sit by myself and listen or find a quiet space.

Every time I start to get worked up over something, I just think to myself,

'Is this going to matter in my life tomorrow, in an hour, in a year?'

Kylie Jenner

What I have found is that the best way to unwind is cooking. You only have two hands.

If you are chopping veggies, you are forcing yourself to put the phone down or step away from the computer.

It's extremely relaxing.

Whitney Wolfe Herd

My personal
hobbies are
reading,
listening to
music,
and
silence.

Edith Sitwell

Adopt the pace
of nature.
Her secret is
PATIENCE.

Ralph Waldo Emerson

If I have something that I'm dealing with that's causing me a lot of stress, my mind goes to **architecture**.
I walk around the yard and start thinking about what I need to do to the house structurally. It's similar to puzzles in a way, like a crossword puzzle or anything else I can put my mind into.
It's a relief to me.

Brad Pitt

Whenever I gaze up at the moon, I feel like I'm on a time machine. **I am back to that precious pinpoint of time, standing on the foreboding – yet beautiful – Sea of Tranquility.** I could see our shining blue planet Earth poised in the **darkness of space.**

Buzz Aldrin

Live as if you were to die tomorrow, learn as if you were to live forever.

Mahatma Gandhi

Remember, it's
… the love you
never see that's
quietly guiding
and boundlessly
supporting you
every step of your
journey's way.

Dwayne 'The Rock' Johnson

As you make your way along life's tumultuous highways, it's important to note that you should always carry a map, have plenty of fuel in the tank, and take frequent rest stops.

Octavia Spencer

It's one of the greatest gifts you can give yourself, to forgive. **FORGIVE EVERYBODY.**

Maya Angelou

I've learned that
I can't have a
    packed work schedule
and a
    packed social schedule
and a
    packed personal life;
I need to just have time to
myself to **sit** and **breathe**
and **unwind**.

Kim Cattrall

Your body is precious, as it houses your mind and spirit.

Inner peace begins with a relaxed body.

Norman Vincent Peale

I found I
could say
things with
**colour and
shapes** that I
couldn't say
any other way.

Georgia O'Keeffe

YOU DON'T ALWAYS NEED A PLAN. Sometimes you just need to breathe, trust, let go and see what happens.

Mandy Hale

Give yourself
time to digitally
detox from
your constantly
connected life,
and **keep your
phone away
from your bed**.

Caroline Ghosn

Relax.
No one
else knows
what they're
doing either.

Unknown

I love the feeling when the whole world has shut down for the day. **I'm left to think and unwind without any interruptions.**

Darren Hayes

Every day,
think as
you wake up,
   'I am fortunate
   to be alive.
   I have a precious
   human life.
   I'm not going to
   waste it.'

Dalai Lama

We do not have to
become heroes overnight.
Just a step at a time,
meeting each
thing that comes up,
seeing it as not as
dreadful as it appears,
discovering that we
have the strengths
to stare it down.

Eleanor Roosevelt

Almost everything will work again if you unplug it for a few minutes. Including you.

Anne Lamott

You have enough.
You do enough.
You are enough.
RELAX.

Unknown

After all,
the wrong road
always leads
somewhere.

George Bernard Shaw